8/2022

ath

Empires

Also by John Balaban

POETRY

Like Family (Red Dragonfly, 2009)

Path, Crooked Path (Copper Canyon Press, 2006)

Locusts at the Edge of Summer: New & Selected Poems
(Copper Canyon Press, 1997, 2003)

Words for My Daughter (Copper Canyon Press, 1991)

Blue Mountain (Unicorn Press, 1982)

After Our War (University of Pittsburgh Press, 1974)

TRANSLATION

Ca Dao Việt Nam: Vietnamese Folk Poetry (Copper Canyon Press, 2003)

Spring Essence: The Poetry of Hồ Xuân Hương (Copper Canyon Press, 2000)

Vietnam: A Traveler's Literary Companion, with Nguyen Qui Duc
(Whereabouts Press, 1996)

NONFICTION

Remembering Heaven's Face: A Story of Rescue in Wartime Vietnam
(University of Georgia Press, 2002)

Vietnam: The Land We Never Knew, photography by Geoffrey Clifford
(Chronicle Books, 1989)

FICTION

Coming Down Again (Simon & Schuster/Fireside, 1989)

The Hawk's Tale (Harcourt Brace Jovanovich, 1988)

Empires

JOHN BALABAN

COPPER CANYON PRESS

PORT TOWNSEND, WASHINGTON

Cover art: Close-up of statues of Nemrud Dagh by baytunc / Getty Images

Copper Canyon Press is in residence at Fort Worden State Park in Port Townsend,
Washington, under the auspices of Centrum. Centrum is a gathering place for
artists and creative thinkers from around the world, students of all ages and back-
grounds, and audiences seeking extraordinary cultural enrichment.

LIBRARY OF CONGRESS CATALOGING-IN-PUBLICATION DATA
Names: Balaban, John, 1943– author.
Title: Empires / John Balaban.
Description: Port Townsend, Washington : Copper Canyon Press, [2019]
Identifiers: LCCN 2019013619 | ISBN 9781556595707 (pbk. : alk. paper)
Classification: LCC PS3552.A44 A6 2019 | DDC 811/.54—dc23
LC record available at https://lccn.loc.gov/2019013619

9 8 7 6 5 4 3 2 FIRST PRINTING

COPPER CANYON PRESS
Post Office Box 271
Port Townsend, Washington 98368
www.coppercanyonpress.org

ACKNOWLEDGMENTS

Earlier versions of some of these poems have appeared in *After Our War*; *American Poets*; *Blackbox Manifold*; *Catamaran*; *Cimarron Review*; *Connecticut Review*; *The Florida Review*; *Folios*; *Granta*; *Great River Review*; *The Hudson Review*; *Isle*; *Little Star*; *Locusts at the Edge of Summer*; *The McNeese Review*; *Narrative Magazine*; *New Letters*; *The New York Review of Books*; *Path, Crooked Path*; *Perfect Dragonfly* (Red Dragonfly Press); *Poet Lore*; *Spring Essence: The Poetry of Hồ Xuân Hương*; *Tigertail*; *Valparaiso Poetry Review*; and *War, Literature, and the Arts*. The Stefan Zweig quotation is from George Prochnik, *The Impossible Exile: Stefan Zweig at the End of the World* (2014). The epigraph for "Cibolero" is from *The Journey of Alvar Nuñez Cabeza de Vaca* (1542), translated by Fanny Bandelier (1905). "Préface en Prose" was translated with Donka Farkas.

Contents

Empires

Our generation has gradually learned the great art of living without security. We are prepared for anything. . . . There is a mysterious pleasure in retaining one's reason and spiritual independence particularly in a period when confusion and madness are rampant.

Stefan Zweig

A FINGER

After most of the bodies were hauled away
and while the FBI and Fire Department and NYPD
were still haggling about who was in charge, as smoke cleared,
the figures in Tyvek suits came, gloved, gowned, masked,
ghostly figures searching rubble for pieces of people,
bagging, then sending the separate and commingled remains
to the temporary morgue set up on site.
This is where the snip of forefinger began its journey.

Not alone, of course, but with thousands of other bits not lost
or barged off with the tonnage for sorting at the city landfill.
A delicate tip, burnt and marked "finger, distal" and sent over
to the Medical Examiner's, where forensic anthropologists
sorted human from animal bones from Trade Center restaurants,
all buried together in the Pompeian effect of incinerated dust.

The bit of finger (that might have once tapped text messages,
potted a geranium, held a glass, stroked a cat, tugged
a kite string along a beach) went to the Bio Lab
where it was profiled, bar-coded, and shelved in a Falcon tube.
Memorial Park — that is to say: the parking lot behind the ME —
droned with generators for the dozens of refrigerated trucks
filling with human debris, while over on the Hudson at Pier 94
families brought toothbrushes or lined up for DNA swabbing.

As the year passed, the unidentified remains were dried out
in a desiccation room — humidity pumped out, heat raised high —
shriveled, then vacuum sealed.

                    But the finger tip had
a DNA match in a swab from her brother. She was English.
30 years old. She worked on the 105th floor of the North Tower.
The Times ran a bio. Friends posted blogs. Her father
will not speak about it. Her mother planted a garden in Manhattan.
In that garden is a tree. Some look on it and feel restored.
Others, when the wind lifts its leaves, want to scream.

AFTER THE INAUGURATION, 2013

Without the shedding of blood, there is no remission of sins.
Epistle to the Hebrews, 9:22

Pulling from the tunnel at Union Station, our train
shunts past DC offices and then crosses the rail bridge
over the tidal Potomac blooming in sweeps of sunlight.
Except for me and two young guys in suits studying
spreadsheets on their laptops, and the tattooed girl
curled asleep across two seats, and the coiffed blonde lady
confined to her wheelchair up front next to piled luggage,
it's mostly black folk, some trickling home in high spirits,
bits of Inaugural bunting and patriotic ribbons
swaying from their suitcase handles on the overhead racks,
all of us riding the *Carolinian* south.

Farther on, where it's suddenly sailboats and gulls
on a nook of the Chesapeake, the banked-up railbed
cuts through miles of swamped pines and cypress
as the train trundles past the odd heron stalking frogs,
or, picking up speed, clatters through open cornfields
where, for a few seconds, staring through the dirty glass,
you can spot turkeys scrabbling the stubble. Farther south,
past Richmond, something like snow or frost glints off a field
and you realize it's just been gleaned of cotton
and this is indeed the South. As if to confirm this fact
to all of us on Amtrak, some latter-day Confederate
has raised the rebel battle-flag in a field of winter wheat.

At dusk, just outside Raleigh, the train slows
and whistles three sharp calls at a crossing in Kittrell, NC.
Along the railroad tracks, under dark cedars, lie graves
of Confederates from Petersburg's nine-month siege, men
who survived neither battle nor makeshift hospital
at the Kittrell Springs Hotel, long gone from the town
where our train now pauses for something up ahead.

Nearby in Oxford, in 1970, a black GI was shot to death.
One of his killers testified: "That nigger committed suicide,
coming in here wanting to four-letter-word my daughter-in-law."
Black vets, just back from Vietnam, set the town on fire.
Off in the night, you could see the flames from these rails
that once freighted cotton, slaves, and armies.

                              Now our Amtrak
speeds by, passengers chatting, or snoozing, or just looking out
as we flick on past the shut-down mills, shotgun shacks, collapsed
tobacco barns, and the evening fields with their white chapels
where "The Blood Done Sign My Name" is still sung, where
the past hovers like smoke or a train whistle's call.

CHRISTMAS EVE AT WASHINGTON'S CROSSING

Omnia reliquit servare rempublicam
Society of the Cincinnati

Out on the freezing Delaware, ice sheets bob the surface, breaking
against granite pilings of the colonial river inn swept by winter storm.

Gusts of snow blow off a sandbar and sink in plunging currents
where a line of ducks paddles hard against the blizzard

as cornfields on the Jersey banks are whisked into bits
of stalks and broken sheaves spinning in the squalls.

This is where, one such Christmas night, the tall courtly general with bad teeth
risked his neck and his rebels to cross the storming river and rout the Hessians

*

What made them think they could succeed? . . . farmers mostly,
leaving homesteads to load cannon into Durham boats

to row into the snowstorm, then march all night to Trenton,
saving the Republic for Valley Forge and victory at Yorktown.

Before crossing, legend says, they assembled in the snow to hear
Paine's new essay about summer soldiers and sunshine patriots.

What words could call us all together now? On what riverbank?
For what common good would we abandon all?

> During this time Castillo saw, on the neck of an Indian, a little buckle
> from a sword belt, and in it was sewed a horseshoe nail. He took it from
> the Indian, and we asked what it was; they said it had come from Heaven.
> We further asked who had brought it, and they answered that some men,
> with beards like ours, had come from Heaven to that river; that they had
> horses, lances and swords, and had lanced two of them.
>
> The Journey of Alvar Nuñez Cabeza de Vaca (1542)

It's 7:00 a.m. in Tecolote, New Mexico,
and the local news on cable
is going on about some woman high on dust
crashing into kids at a crossing. Meanwhile,
out on the edge of the high prairie,
up by I-25, the inmates are rising off
their roosts at San Miguel county jail
where the jail log reads like catechism:

> Criminal Sexual Penetration in the first degree. Assault with
> the intent to commit violent felony. False imprisonment.
> Extortion. Unlawful taking of a motor vehicle. Conspiracy.
> Burglary of a structure. Contributing to the delinquency
> of a minor. Kidnapping. Conspiracy to commit Aggravated
> Battery. Aggravated DWI (7th offense). Possession of
> drug paraphernalia. Driving on suspended revoked license.
> Probation Violation: Possession of marijuana, Possession of
> Methamphetamine. Aggravated stalking. Aggravated battery
> on household member, resisting, evading, violation of a
> restraining order, obstructing an officer. Vehicular Homicide,
> Aggravated DUI, Open Container, Reckless driving. Assault
> with a deadly weapon. Assault with intent to commit a
> violent felony, with intent to commit mayhem.

The key word here is "mayhem," spreading through
the internet airwaves across the vast Llano Estacado
where mountains break into mesas and scrub,
dotted with piñon, cut by arroyos and twisty creeks
and a web of old footpaths made by ancestors.

And where the internet's thousand channels
are offering their social contracts, so
whether you are watching from prison, or at home
in your double-wide, or in the sleep cab of your semi,
or in your townhouse at the city's edge, or at Urgent Care,
the local laundromat, or in a bar that never closes,
wherever you are watching, you are probably just sitting
(and doing this a lot) tuned to hucksters selling
vacuum cleaners and Jesus, channel by channel:
#9012: Puppy Pooping in the House?
#9013: Thick Hair Guaranteed
#9014: Rev. Run's Sunday Suppers
#9015: Suffer from Lower Back Pain?
Mayhem being confusion turned to violence or lassitude.

But whether in the lockup looking out,
or among the hardworking folk of the Llano
in adobe-and-stone compounds and corrals
in, say, Ojitos Frios, Tecolote, or Villanueva,
when you see the rain dropping its dark curtains
over the vast plain, some Spenglerian twinge of memory
must arrive . . . of the massive adobe pueblo at Pecos,
of Coronado with his armored men on horses,
or, later, as the centuries stood still and Spanish dreams collapsed,
of trading with Comanches and learning to hunt buffalo
charging bareback into the stampeding herd with lowered lance,
shoving it into a thundering beast until it stumbled and crashed down
with all its wealth of meat, tallow, bone, and hide. A barrel
of buffalo tongues for the Viceroy in Mexico. *Cibolero,*
Buffalo Hunter. From *cíbola,* Spanish for "bison," from Zuni, *tzibola.*
Cibola, the city of gold that was never found.

GODS AND EMPIRE

I. XENOPHANES FLEES BEFORE THE PERSIANS

> If horses and oxen had hands and could draw pictures,
> their gods would look remarkably like horses and oxen.
> Xenophanes of Colophon, ca. 570–480 BCE

All day we trudged north along the Aegean, cold rain
squalling, whipping up whitecaps, churning sandbars,
eating the beach, rocking pines, hissing sand-sleet.

But the hardest storms came at night, scouring us
huddled in dunes as strikes of violet light flashed
off the cliffs, igniting our faces when thunder boomed

and we were caught out not by pursuers, but by the gods
the soldiers whined, as they crouched under leather shields,
like dogs in the deafening downpour. By morning,

the sea was calm and we saw the sun and moon
together. So close they almost touched. The shoreline
was now rain-rinsed, wind-brushed, smoothed,

and all about strewn with the crania of huge jellyfish
fading like lanterns in the sunlit air, under a rainbow,
dying like gods in throes of contemplation, or so I jested,

a philosopher fleeing with soldiers, perplexing them
with "She whom you call Iris, or rainbow, is merely cloud.
Sing a dirge for her," I said, "if you think she is divine,"

adding we were weakened by superstition and by luxury
like the Lydians oblivious to threat, idling about in purple robes,
boastful, comely, proud, each anointed with rich perfumes.

Soon we heard trumpets drifting off the headlands.
Soon we saw the Medes' war chariots, their sacrificial knives, heard
their prophets screaming. Saw their crudely fashioned gods.

The following are fit topics for conversation for men reclining on a soft
couch by the fire in the winter season, . . . Who are you, and what is
your family? Where is your land, my friend? How old were you when the
Medes invaded your land?

Fragments of Xenophanes

What does it matter if the women
of Colophon are no longer given
to stroll the streets in flowing, sea-purple robes?

That the pipe no longer leads seductive odes
sung in the voluptuous Lydian modes?
That Medes now temper their swords on our hearths?

Walking on Colophon's foggy shore at night
I once was the center of a circle of sight.
The wheel of a chariot has one locus.

My eye circumscribed the radius of the real.
Behind me the fog cloaked what it revealed
while before me it opened like the folds of a robe.

Strained with a vision, my self began to breathe.
I was twenty. My poetry recited along the Aegean
when we heard the brass trumpets of the Asian tribes.

Now I am an amusement to strangers, drinking
their wine at banquets. For sixty-seven years thinking
my thoughts, while tossed restlessly up and down Greece.

Such is Xenophanes, aged *rhapsode* and lover of wisdom,
who looked into all things of earth and heaven
and made of them a song, sung in a time of barbarians.

POETRY READING BY THE BLACK SEA

Often, gates shut, safe inside the walls,
we gathered arrows fallen in the streets.
Ovid, *Tristia* V, X: 21–22

A breeze riffles in from the beach
stirring poplar catkins, woolly stuff
drifting the town in flurries, searching

the air like syllables of poetry while
we perch on the stones of this Roman bath
listening to poetry, the delicate thing which lasts.

Here at empire's edge, boys, silly with love,
chatted idly by the pools. Merchants,
trading amphorae of oil and Lydian dye,

cursed thin profits, cruel seas, lost ships.
Now seagulls flap and squawk on broken walls
scurfed with weeds and the royal poppy.

Greek and Roman, Getae, Thracian, Bulgar,
Slavs, Avars, Goths, Celts, Tatars, Huns,
Arabs, Turks, Russians, and, now, the US Navy.

Not far from here, one frigid winter in Tomis,
an aging Ovid, exiled by Augustus,
donned a helmet to defend the ramparts

as Thracian horsemen circled the frozen marsh,
their long hair tinkling with chinks of ice,
shooting poisoned arrows into the walled city

killing the boy who attended the old poet,
the boy he paid to massage his skin, there
in "the last place," among barbarians

two thousand years ago. And, now, acacias
fragrance our evening as poplar fluff floats
over imperial rubble. "Only poetry lasts."

"THE SMELL OF AUTUMN RAIN . . ."

from the Romanian of Benjamin Fundoianu

Herța, 1917

The smell of autumn rain and hay hung
about the village, soaking the lungs.
Girls dawdled on the dirty streets
which filled with silence each evening.
The postman shuffled by, slow, hooded, deaf.
Hay wagons — chased by rain — had left
and silence settled and grew moldy as
simple folk whispered Yiddish in their homes.
The drizzle snuffed a gaslight with a hiss,
hissed back by geese waddling to a house.
Leaves were rotting in the old bell's mouth.
We heard these awkward autumn sounds:
the mailcoach rattling in from Dorohoi,
the oxen rising from the bare soil,
bellowing, heads back as if to suck the sky.
The village bellowed back with reddish eyes.

PRÉFACE EN PROSE

from the French of Benjamin Fondane

I am talking to you, my opposite Others.
I am talking man to man
with that bit of myself which remains a man,
that bit of my voice still stuck in my throat.
My blood is on the streets, may it — oh, may it not —
cry out for vengeance.
The hunter's horn is sounded. The hounds are on the track.
So let me now speak to you in words we once shared
though few still make sense.

A day will come, for sure, when thirst quenched,
we will have gone beyond memory, and death
will have finished hatred's work, and I
will have become a bunch of nettles under your feet.
But, look, you need to know I had a face like you.
A mouth that prayed, like you.

When a speck of dust or a dream
entered my eyes, they wept a little salt.
And when a nasty thorn pricked my skin
it bled red blood, just like yours.
And, yeah, like you, I was cruel, and hungered
for tenderness, for power, money, pleasure, and pain.
Just like you I was mean, filled with anguish,
reliable enough at peace, drunk in victory,
and staggering and worn in times of failure.

And, sure, I was a man like other men
nourished by bread, by dreams, and by despair,
and sure, I loved, wept, hated, and suffered.
I bought flowers and sometimes I skipped on my rent.
On Sundays, I might go to the countryside and fish,
to catch, under God's eye, his fish of irreality
and bathe in the river that sang in the bulrushes

and eat fries in the evening. Later, I'd go back
and sleep, my heart worn out and lonely,
full of pity for myself, full of pity for mankind,
searching, searching in vain on a woman's body
for that impossible peace we lost once in a great orchard
with the tree of life flowering at its heart.

Like you I read all the newspapers, the books,
and understood nothing of the world,
understood nothing about men,
though often I may have claimed to.
When death, when death came, perhaps
I pretended to understand but, really,
(I can tell you now)
when all of death entered my astonished eyes
I was stunned by how little I had understood.
Did you understand it any better?

And yet . . . no!
I wasn't a man like you.
You were not born on the road.
No one ever dropped your children into a sewer
like blind kittens, you never had to wander
from city to city, tracked by cops.

You never knew calamity at dawn,
or cattle cars, or bitter sobs of humiliation
when accused of a crime you never committed,
a murder without a body, or had to change your name
and face, not to have an abused name or a face that served
as a spittoon.

But a day will come, for sure, when this poem
will lie before you, asking nothing.
Leave it. Leave it. It's just an outcry.
You can't turn that into a poem.
(Will I have time to polish this?)
But when you tread on this clutch of nettles
that was once me, reading this in some other century
like an outdated story, remember that I was innocent
and that like you, mortals of your day, I too
had a face marked by anger, and by pity, and by joy.

A man's face, quite simply.

Benjamin Fondane was a poet and philosopher, born Beniamin Wechsler in Iaşi,
Romania, in 1898. He was the son of Isac Wechsler, a small-tradesman from Herţa
(in Bucovina), and Adela, sister of the Jewish scholars Elias Wilhelm and Moses
Schwarzfeld. In Romania, before taking off for Paris and avant-garde renown, he
wrote under the name Fundoianu. "Préface en Prose," probably his last poem,
was written in 1944, the year the Nazis took him and his sister first to Drancy
and then to Auschwitz, where they perished.

THE ALIBI

from the Romanian of Ştefan Augustin Doinaş

We can't do anything in this world without risking the deaths of others.
Camus, *The Plague*

Endlessly, on the fields, in archways,
on the street, in woods, on altars, in bed,
day and night, someone commits murder.

Was I present? The bulging eye
clouds over and shuts. The hand denies
it was an accomplice.

Was I there?
A blotch of blood upon the brow
is passed from father to son.

I saw the stab and the collapse.
I heard the cry. And then
the knife, dripping, blinded me.

But I saw him. I know he is among us,
but I cannot say his name. What name
will fit all the many children,

sick on games and jokes,
who murder their childhood?
Lovers enter the thigh

of the madman, and die in quicklime.
A flock of crows wheels
about their bodies. And all is hopeless.

What flag shall we fly over the city?
Where shall we flee? All roads are cut.
Like God Who Is Everywhere,

we had a hand in all these deaths.
Accomplices — yet whose? Stuff my mouth
with rags so I can't speak.

The unborn of our honored race
sleep soundly. They have an alibi.

RETURNING AFTER OUR WAR

> *But in Indo-China I drained a magic potion, a loving-cup which I have
> shared since with many retired colon and officers of the Foreign Legion whose
> eyes light up at the mention of Saigon and Hanoi.*
>
> Graham Greene, *Ways of Escape*

I. SAIGON

The other night, I went with friends to see the Saigon River where
it loops past the venerable Majestic Hotel still standing on the river-
bank at the end of the modernized, old downtown. From the hotel's
top floor balcony, we looked across to the Nhà Bè side from where,
back in the American days, rockets were sometimes launched at the
city from the mangrove swamps across the way. We stood awhile
saying nothing just watching the boats chugging slowly behind dim
bow lights as a full moon floated above the river.

During the war, the street behind the Majestic was — architecturally
speaking — still a colonial avenue of small shops, GI bars, cafés,
Maxim's nightclub (still there), and green-shuttered *appartements*
with yellow, stuccoed walls leaking blotches of mildew. Now it's a
dazzle of luxury hotels and skyscrapers. Downtown Saigon is nearly
unrecognizable but, every now and then, my taxi would turn a
corner, stirring up a memory of some distant encounter . . . an
argument in a government ministry, a flower market where I once
bought a pair of finches, or simply our corner cigarette stall where a
gold-toothed old lady sold Marlboros tapped up with marijuana.

Behind the Majestic, the old Graham Greene apartment is gone,
though one remembers the man who prepared Greene's opium,
still climbing the creaky wooden steps into the early '70s to serve
Americans with his valise of pipes. Now, after many re-inventions,
it's become a garish complex of glass and metal called "Katina"
as the global imperium changed hands over the decades and the
Rue Catinat became Tự Do or Freedom Street, and then, after our
war, Đồng Khởi, or Great Uprising, and Saigon became Ho Chi
Minh City.

2. THE OPIUM PILLOW

That night I woke from one of those short deep opium sleeps, ten minutes long, that seem a whole night's rest....
Graham Greene, *The Quiet American*

A cool ceramic block, a brick
just larger than one's cheek,

cream-colored, bordered in blue,
a finely crackled glaze, but smooth,

a hollow bolster on which to lay
one's head before it disappears

in curls of acrid opium fumes
slowly turning in the tropical room

lit by a lampwick's resinous light
snaking shadows up a wall.

The man who served us with his pipes,
with tarred and practiced hands,

worked a heated wad of rosin
"cooked the color of a cockroach wing"

into the pinhole of the fat pipebowl.
He said, "Draw." One long pull

that drew in combers of smoke rolling
down the lungs like the South China Sea,

crashing on the mind's frail shell
that rattled, then wallowed, and filled with sand.

★

I woke up to animal groans . . .
Down in the stairwell Flynn and Stone

were beating up a young thief
who had broken in to steal their bikes

bucking an M16 against the kid's ear
then punching him in the stomach with its butt

before they bum-rushed him out the door
doubled over and wheezing for air.

I stammered *no* in a syllable that rose
like a bubble lifting off the ocean floor.

Ten days later, they were dead. Flynn
and Stone, who dealt in clarities of force,

who motorcycled out to report the war,
shot at a roadblock on Highway 1.

Nearly all those Saigon friends are gone now.
Gone like smoke. Like incense.

> for Tom and John Steinbeck, Crystal Eastin Erhart Steinbeck Brown,
> Steve Erhart, Sean Flynn, and Louise and Dana Stone

3. ABANDONED HOUSE, SAIGON

Two swallows fly in a broken window, sweeping under
yellow orchids tumbling from the rotted frame.

The ghost up there has stopped her complaining
while out in the rain below a tarp, a girl selling soup

squats by the curb slicing tiny hoops of chili,
piling little heaps of red on a white dish.

Did the ghost upstairs learn English or French?
Where did she intend to go? Why does she linger?

How her lips must burn when her fingers brush them.
One swallow darts out the darkened window

while over in LA, stuck in traffic, a Vietnamese guy
remembers this street, the vendor, the house lying almost empty.

One evening, I went for a walk in downtown Hanoi, around its lake surrounded by ancient banyans and plots of tropical plants, with its old temple on an island out in the middle. On weekend evenings, this whole area of the city is blocked off to traffic and everywhere dance groups — tango, ballet, ballroom, rock — dance to loudspeaker recordings or, in some cases, live bands, including a brass band that blares swing to the crowd this evening as one woman sprawls on her back on a nearby bench and sleeps, oblivious to the crowd around her and Duke Ellington's "Take the 'A' Train."

Farther along, a guy is playing "Despacito" on an electrified, two-string đàn cò, while little kids zip around the opened streets on remote-controlled electric cars, chased after by yappy little dogs pausing only to sniff particularly enticing shoes in the milling crowds . . . *Several million of them died in the war.*

But now the streets are packed with strolling families, and I am so glad for them.

sleeping in the heart of Hanoi
where the elderly gather at dawn
for tai chi, windmilling their arms
and chatting as they walk the lakeside paths.

Goodbye to the feathery Hoàng Điệp trees
leaning over the water toward the little island
with its shrine for the ancient hero
who gave back the sacred sword.

And goodbye to the old woman
sitting zazen every morning by the water's edge
as the lake watches her with its glassine
sentient eye, and sometimes blinks.

THREE MEN DANCING ON A RIVER SHORE

Ch'ing Dynasty Serving Platter, Blue-and-White Porcelain

In the background, you can see the city they left behind
when they crossed the river to dance on this shore,
three gentlemen in mandarin robes and scruffy beards
now jigging on the sand under pines and willows
accompanied by musicians on trumpet, flute, and drum
and one plying a squeeze-box of some kind
for these scholars waving their hands above their heads,
kicking up sand and celebrating friendship, their dharma bridge
for getting to the other side, however briefly.

Three men dancing. Not drunk, just immensely amused
knowing that soon enough there would be only the wind
shushing its sad music along an empty shore.

for Tim Buckley and Tracy McCallum

SHOWGIRL

Like Mary of Egypt, her patron saint,
she roamed the desert and her travels weren't easy,
getting to Taos by way of The Sands and The Copacabana
after running off from the chorus line in Vegas
with $400 in her hip pocket. Before her escape
she watched an A-bomb blast out in the desert
with Jimmy Durante, who liked to call her Richard.

She said
she loved the revues, her rhinestones and ostrich plumes.
Nevermind the night she got tipsy and mocked a mobster
who followed her to her hotel room with a tire iron,
shoved her on the bed, and pressed the greasy metal
against her perfect face.

Oh, such a long way from the Catfish and Pee Dee rivers
and the small Georgia town where her father ran a store and
where, boy-crazy at 15 and hot-to-trot, she ran off with an older kid
and was married for a few weeks
until it was annulled.

Years later, in Taos, she'd sit with her cigarettes in the cool dark
of her adobe art gallery and joke about the men she liked,
their mayhem and punch-ups, the painter who shot a guy
in the nuts for coming on to his son, her aging Greek boyfriend
who owned the hotel on the plaza where he lived with his mother,
the antics of actors, writers, and provocateurs. The painters
whose early work she showed until they got famous or dead.

Little explains her eye for art,
her elegant prose in *Art in America*, her fierce
enigmatic feuds, the rubble of her romances, her

melancholy life alone
with Pinky, her dyspeptic cat painted by Fritz Scholder, or
her languorous voice sifting through smoke across her crepuscular room
like mist through Georgia pines.

for Tally Richards (1928–2008)

REMEMBERING ELLING EIDE (1935–2012)

Sent to Tu Fu
From Beneath the City Wall at Sandhill

Why have I come here after all?
To rest in retreat by the Sandhill wall.
By the side of the wall are some ancient trees
with the sounds of autumn both night and day.
But I can't get drunk on the wines of Lu,
and my feelings are wasted in the songs of Ch'i.
My thoughts of you like the River Wen
go rolling southward endlessly.

Elling Eide translation from the Chinese of Li Po

Around dawn the hurricane died and neighbors crept out to see
their snapped trees, lawns littered with leaf mash and roof bits
blown into heaps with siding, broken birds, and snakes.

By afternoon, chainsaws were screaming
in the sickening August heat and bulldozers began
to scrape the rotting tonnage from the streets.

That's when Elling drove over from Sarasota
in his old VW van packed with candles, with
dog food, cat food, flashlights and batteries,

jugs of water, a frozen cake dripping icing, crackers,
caviar, a chilled case of Tsingtao beer, chainsaw blades,
and tropical trees to plant the place again.

In a few years, our new ylang-ylang rose
thirty feet, unfurling long yellow blossoms
to fill our evenings with attar of Chanel.

And so it went with Elling's palms,
his gumbo limbo, Cuban guanabana,
papaya, bananas, and bamboo, the house

again shaded, overhung with bougainvillea,
trellised in passion vine, scented by gardenia,
by Burmese orchids that drink the humid air.

Once again, parrots flock the sea grape for its fruit,
the "birds assembling as if to audit the Dharma"
as Elling once translated Li Po's lines. And now,

like the Taoist poet, Elling has gone off somewhere
and our thoughts for him "like the River Wen
go rolling southward endlessly."

FINISHING UP THE NOVEL AFTER SOME DELAY

I followed a stream plunging out of the jungle
through a spill of boulders broken loose
from twisting roots of pandanus trees.

A sandfly cloud see-sawed the mudflat
and I turned to go the other way
through thickets splattered in sunshine
where green rollers screamed and bobbed in bamboo
through cool palms as high as my head.
The earth, spongy; the air, damp.

A blue-tailed babbler screeched high up
above the chattering stream. Downriver,
some women waded pools with dip nets.
Their kids chased fish in the weirs.
I passed unseen behind the jungle wall.

In the great shade of the triple canopy
screwpines walked on hairy stilts below teak
and towering coffin trees, their blue-green trunks
festooned with cascades of yellow orchids.
Leaf monkeys hid in banyans.

Finally I saw them resting on a knoll:
My poor characters had been through a lot.
Roberts sat and rubbed his bare torn feet.
Fay — in sweat-stained blouse from Portobello Road,
her neck and hands all raw with scabies —
leaned back to have her hair combed out by Mai
who shared her prison cell for seven months.
Squinting her eyes, Fay faced the healing sun.

Calling would have scared them. I stepped out gently.
Mai yelped "Hey," and Roberts slowly smiled.
I was awfully glad they were glad to see me.
When I left they said I'd never come back.

FOR CHÖGYAM TRUNGPA, THE ELEVENTH TRUNGPA TULKU, WHO FLED TIBET FOR INDIA WHEN THE CHINESE INVADED

Chased by Chinese troops, the monks
blinked like owls in the sun sheen

abandoning their burning temple
where the obdurate slumped over altars

with bullet-hole Third Eyes oozing
gunpowder and pineal, black blood.

With blizzards choking the high passes
they huddled in cliff caves

while trusting you to lead them through,
a 600-year-old boy,

who was *coming from behind his back*
and was *going in the direction he faced.*

The Chinese prowled behind like wolves
as snow squalls filled your tracks.

As weeks passed, peasants and monks
boiled their saddlebags and ate them,

drove yaks ahead to breach the snowdrifts
and then men when the beasts perished.

By a blue lake in a Himalayan valley
where only the yeti had ever stood upright

you meditated on the dharma path.
Rinpoche, I glimpsed you once

hailing a cab on Madison Avenue.
Where were you going?

THE USES OF POETRY

Writing poems about writing poems
is like rolling bales of hay in Texas.
Nothing but the horizon to stop you.
Ruth Stone, "Always on the Train"

The poets descend like locusts
wings filmy, bright, whirring ambitions

with mandible greed for green expanses,
for tended lushest leaf, all foliage,

the fury of their wingbeats
sickening and familiar:

a swarm out of Egypt
eating everything in their path.

But some sing. The Cicadidae,
burrowed deep in dark earth for years,

crawl out to creep up trees, eating nothing,
inching toward sunlight,

abandoning their husks, pitching out
cascades of calls high in the treetops.

A VISIT FROM HIS MUSE

*. . . the goddesses said to me — the Muses of Olympus, daughters of Zeus
who holds the aegis:* Shepherds of the wilderness, wretched
things of shame, mere bellies, we know how to speak many
false things as though they were true; but we know, when
we will, to utter true things

*. . . and they plucked and gave me a rod, a shoot of sturdy olive, a mar-
velous thing, and breathed into me a divine voice to celebrate things that
shall be and things that were aforetime; and they bade me sing of the
race of the blessed gods that are eternally, but ever to sing of themselves
both first and last.*

Hesiod, *Theogony,* 1.22

"Honey," she said, "well, here we are again."
  She plucked at a hole in her panty hose.
"A run-down room in a backwater town
  and you, love, want to dance in light."

He shuffled his shoes and muttered
he was "eating salads and laying off the booze"
and hoped she'd bite, agree to stick around
and set things right in the wretched room.

"Baby" (she said) "you even know what you want?
'Cause maybe you need another kind of girl.
  You can't make time with your Muse. Oh, my."
  She fluffed the pillows, smacked the sheets for fleas.

At dawn the doves were cooing on the ledge.
A fading moon slid softly from his bed.

DOWN UNDER

To the very last minute of his life, Australian John Balaban, 29, couldn't
get on with people. Even as he was being led to the execution chamber in
Adelaide Prison on Wednesday . . . , he snarled at the chaplain, who was
trying to give him last-minute comfort, "Why don't you shut up?"
Adelaide *Messenger* (August 26, 1953)

Well, you've got to love him, my doppelgänger
sticking it to the chaplain like Meursault in *The Stranger.*
Yet, after clapping for him, I got a chill, reading on
that after he "arrived in Australia from Romania in 1951"
my double-goer strangled his wife and little son,
and slashed up a prostitute named Zora, not to mention
the Hungarian girl, Reva Kwas, back in Paris.

Perhaps I should make clear that I was just a little kid myself
in a suburb of Philadelphia when all that happened in Australia.
True, my parents were Romanian, but there's an entire village
called Balabaneşti in the rolling farmlands near the Black Sea
where I bet half the men are named for Saint John, or Michael.
Still, it's odd to see your name stolen by someone who
Is underneath the grave, where do inhabit
The shadows of all forms that think and live,
as Shelley wrote, after seeing his own double
before drowning in the Gulf of La Spezia.

Even the Shelley maid, Mrs. Williams, saw the double.
"Good God!" she cried, "can Shelley have leapt from the wall?
Where can he be gone?" Nobody likes to run into them,
creepy with twilight, lurching from the shadows to spook us.
Does everyone have one? I recall another John Balaban,
a road-raged wacko who attacked a carload of young drunks
on a snowy night, hooking one arm in the driver's window
and dragged along by their car skidding the ice-crusted road
as he wailed punch after punch onto the driver lurching away,
everyone in the car screaming as he hung on, his legs kicking
to find footing, still punching, until the tires finally got traction
and the car sped off, dropping him facedown in the slush.

I mean, where did *he* come from? I guess I could say
that was my doppelgänger, not me, but that just confuses
the supernatural with having a bad temper, and either explanation
is not worth a strand of poor Zora's blood-caked hair.

Nonetheless, Achilles, trying to explain his famous wrath
in the *Iliad*, simply says "*Atē* consumed me."
Atē, Zeus's oldest daughter and thus a goddess,
specialized in blinding mortals and gods to
their better selves, their other selves, their good selves,
and got herself banished from Olympus to live
down under, deity to doppelgängers, sending them,
now and then, from their land of shadows into ours.

THE POET RETIRES

I have known the inexorable sadness of pencils,
Neat in their boxes, dolor of pad and paper-weight
Theodore Roethke, "Dolor"

When the poet said goodbye to the workaday world
along with all its yammer and strife,
he took off for his cabin in the woods
with no regrets. He had his books. Looking out
across the autumn woods, the stirring branches
seemed to make his thoughts come alive and rise
on the wind to greet him. After a long walk
by the creek that ran down past the cabin,
he poured himself a drink, and put on a record.
Instead of his usual Charlie Parker, he put on Iggy Pop
reciting a poem from the *Avenue B* album:
"My home and study meant more to me . . .
I wanted to find a balance between joy and dignity
on my way out. Above all, I didn't want
to take any more shit. Not from anybody."

Nature is at times a shameless playwright.

John Barth, *The Floating Opera*

TIDE POOL

Here the ancient lava slid into the sea,
hissed up steam clouds, then cooled into stone

making a moonscape in the volcanic shelf
pocked with basins, cracked by runnels

where tides chafe canyons day and night
scooping out clear shallow pools,

sand-bottomed cisterns, where sun shaft
and tide-froth ply their metaphors.

At the pool's edge, a hermit crab with ivory claw,
pop-dot blue eyes, and strawberry whiskers

sidles off under some dead shell.
In the tidal rinse, blue neon fingerlings

flit between the rocks. Fiddlers swim away
at the shift of a shadow and deeper down

beneath wrinkles of light in the tide-washed crooks
the ink-purple urchins wait for whatever.

A sun and a moon, but a fishbowl nonetheless
for little lives in their amorous wriggles,

for the crashing sea punching holes below the shelf
flushing innocent worlds, leaving only

a stone stage for watery dramas beneath the sky,
an existential entertainment, an opera mimicking

our desire for an imagined home, in a place
forever perishing, a place to live.

ANNIE'S STARLING

The *baby* starling, fallen from its nest,
the blind fledgling Annie found in the backyard
flopping around without a clue about up or down,
a bald, pin-feathered, blue-lidded, bulgy-eyed *Sturnus vulgaris*,
an "urban pest," whose noisy ancestors got to New York
in 1890, and flocked across America, Alaska to Mexico.

Always a sucker for outcasts, Annie cupped it to her chest
and called her daughter, who said try feeding it cat food.

By spring, it was flying around the house, sitting on her shoulder
when she read, or wrote, or did the dishes, refusing to leave
even when starlings chattered outside, the front door left open,
as if Annie were St. Ives and the bird had something to tell her.

And when Annie was packing her car for the drive from Eugene
to San Francisco, where Joe was living on his houseboat and
things were looking good for the two of them, the bird flew
out from the house and into the car and would not shoo, but
settled in for the car ride, 500 miles . . . to enjoy its week
on Richmond Bay, and the long ride back to Eugene.

Maybe the bird was just looking Joe over, because it took off
right after that trip. Maybe it was saying, "Make a new home."

Anyway, this is how I remember the story.

AT NORA'S HOUSE, SHEPARD'S ROOST, ATLANTIC BEACH, NC

Out beyond the porthole above the kitchen sink
a line of pelicans skims a breaker, wing tips

brushing the tattering crest as if to feel the herring
running inside the green lung of the recoiling wave

scales flashing as the school flips a turn and the roller
rises then collapses along this south-facing beach.

All morning, terns plunging up plumes of sea-spray
have been flying off with mullet wriggling in their bills.

Last night, as dials of dune grass marked time in the sand
and while the summer's clock of stars circled the Pole

a fox curled in a hollow, snug in the sea-oat dunes.
A huge green turtle struggled ashore to nest.

In the house's cool cellar, Shep's rowboat — dry-docked
and drifting with the years — still trails a wake of sunlight

and salt marsh, crab pots, duck blinds, bay chop
slapping boat chines, and Nora and the girls, laughing.

WAITING FOR THE PAINTER TO RETURN

All the trees were drinking from the fog
spilling over hillsides — the pines, and

farther down, an apple orchard, gnarled
and abandoned. Along the creek

the acacias flushed yellow, as gophers
gnawed around under the old pasture.

Her jasmine continued to climb the porch
and seemed willing to consider spring.

Above the barn studio, its tin roof was quieted
by the fog, and listening as her paintings

offered each other their critiques, everything
waiting for the gate to open, her car to pull in.

for Susan Jane Adams

A MIAMI MOMENT

Just home from work, he's sitting
by the patio pond, watching the koi
write their slow signatures.

Beside him: the *Miami Herald*
gathering humid air, a glass of wine,
and the cigar he left last night.

A flock of parrots mutters
in the sea-grape tree. The ylang-ylang
has put on its evening perfume

and soon the yard will smell like Chanel.
Inside his daughter is baking cookies
and his wife is taking a pre-dinner snooze.

He jumps up screaming.
Inside, they yell "What? What!?"
and run out to see him pointing up

at maybe fifty vultures circling,
wings underlit by the setting sun
in a swirl of slow turning light.

The magic in the realism
never far away.

ANNA AKHMATOVA SPENDS THE NIGHT ON
MIAMI BEACH

Well, her book, anyway. The Kunitz volume
left lying on a bench, the pages
a bit puffy by morning, flushed with dew,
riffled by sea breeze, scratchy with sand
—the paperback with the 1930s photo
showing her in spangled caftan, its back cover
calling her "star of the St. Petersburg circle
of Pasternak, Mandelstam, and Blok,
surviving the Revolution and two World Wars."

So she'd been through worse . . .
the months outside Lefortovo prison
waiting for a son who was already dead, watching
women stagger and reel with news of executions,
one mother asking, "Can you write about this?"
Akhmatova thinking, then answering, "Yes."

If music lured her off the sandy bench
to the clubs where men were kissing,
être outré wouldn't have concerned her much
nor the vamps sashaying in leather.
Decadence amid art deco fit nicely
with her black dress, chopped hair, Chanel cap.
What killed her was the talk, the empty eyes,
which made her long for the one person in ten thousand
who could say her name, who could take her home,
giving her a place between Auden and Apollinaire
to whom she could describe her night's excursion
amid the loud hilarities, the consuming hungers,
arriving toward the end of the American era.

In the desert there is nothing but the presence of Allah.

Arab proverb

CHASING OUT THE DEMONS

We wanted to confess our sins but there were no takers.
White clouds refused to accept them, and the wind
Was too busy visiting sea after sea.
　　　　　Czesław Miłosz, "At a Certain Age"

A bad case. Alone in the canyon,
screaming and charging a dirtbike
at the sandstone cliffs, he squinted
behind his wire-rim glasses
as the bugs splashed green and he bucked
across cottonwood roots and rubble
at breakneck speed, on a whining bike,
skidding to stops at the canyon walls.

At night, zipped in a sleeping bag,
he squirmed like a chrysalis under the moon
while the wind searched the willows
and the creek plunked into little pools
where trout batted at fireflies.

The two Yuroks came in his sleep:
two ghosts, pulses of wind and moonlight,
squatting beside him on the balls of their feet.
He shouted when the woman smoothed his hair.
And then they were gone, and he cried.
Sobbed hard because it was goodbye,
goodbye to the spirit that raged in him by day
and now was traveling across the canyon creek
led off by the ghosts, the two
who had come to calm him.

He sat up that night by the dark, cold water,
wrapped in a blanket, listening to the creek,
breaking his reverie only once
to cup his hands and draw to his lips
the moon rocking on the clear water.

　　　for Tim Buckley

COYOTE PAST SUNSET

Finally, after a whole day of tailing trucks,
the highways loud with tire whine and bumper glare,
he got onto a blacktop running south to Mexico,
just him on the road, and off in the desert, dust devils
swirling over greasewood and yucca spikes,
ruffling the vultures sunning on fence posts
and whipping up grit around the odd horse
or pronghorns grazing with cattle, as he sped on
past hundreds of miles of barbed-wire fences.

After dusk, when he was nearly there, the moon
rose over the Chinati Mountains lighting cottonwoods
as he crossed the dry arroyo at the town limits.
Everything felt good, he thought. It was good to be alone.
That's when he saw the coyote trotting the berm,
turning its head to give him a haggard look, licking the air,
then padding out toward the high desert, past a house
with its TV flickering, the family at its meal.

EL MERCADO

You know on walking in, seeing
the big display of flyswatters
next to the dusty ketchup bottles,
the aisle of chips and salsa, the corn dogs,
the radishes aging in their bins,
the rotting avocados

. . . know that few pass through here, that few
stop in this high desert town by the border,
and that whatever you've come looking for
you probably won't find.

EL CEMENTERIO DE LA MERCED

*The likeness of the heart is that of a feather blown about by the wind
in the desert.*
Abu Musa al-Ash'ari, Vol. 1, Book 1, Hadith 88

Some pronghorn antelope have gotten through the barbed-wire fence
and into the graveyard, looking for shade in the cedars and pines,

or perhaps just fooled by the plastic flowers, and now are grazing
among the Spanish headstones and pointed, wooden crosses,

lifting and dropping their horned heads, their parched white faces,
as they amble by a gravelly plot for three women, buried together:

Elizabeth, Dolores, and Addie, the last to go, at 80, in 2002.
Why do they share a gravesite, with their stones inscribed in English?

Why aren't they in the Anglo graveyard across the fence?
Back in town, I asked some older women but no one knew them.

So, who buried them? No such names are in the local phone book.
Nor on the graves nearby, here in the ghostly Texan *despoblado*.

LOOKING FOR THE LIGHTS

Around midnight, his pickup shut off, engine still ticking,
parked off a road running through ancient lava flows

dotted with mesquite and ocotillo, with cactus and yucca,
he listened to a javelina pack snuffling nearby in a dry wash

in the cool dry night air pulling up from Pinto Canyon,
from the Chinati Mountains just above the border,

not a ranch house light for miles, just Orion stalking a full moon,
as he leaned against his dusty tailgate looking for the Light,

that is, the Marfa Lights that wink above the desert brush,
the Lights that local Indians took for star people visiting Earth,

and early ranchers tried to ride down, thinking them campfires
of Mexican or Apache rustlers from across the Rio Grande.

★

When he first heard it barreling down the blacktop, lights flashing,
he figured it for an ambulance speeding to rescue some rancher

but after it pulled to a screeching halt and wheeled its headlights on him,
roof-rack lights strobing blue-and-red across the road and berm, and

a voice called from behind the driver's opened door, and then the spotlight
flicked on, blinding him, he knew it was the Border Patrol and, most likely,

there was a gun on him as well. He explained he was an American
and that he was here looking for the Lights. "The what?"

"The Marfa Lights," he said. They had a nice talk after that, but
across the roadway in the night. So he never actually *saw* the agent,

who said he had never seen the Lights himself but knew people who had,
before driving off, leaving him to desert prairie and streams of stars.

BACK THEN

looking for some peace of mind
was like searching for a cricket in a field.
He'd head out, following his best directions
only to drive around from noon to nightfall
past bogs and cornfields and tangly woods.
His car would get stuck, or the battery die
and he would have to hump it to a farmhouse to call for a tow.
Back in town, he would sit at the bar with a beer,
wondering why the locals were lying,
and slapping mosquitoes whining at his ear.
He had all the right gear, just couldn't get there.

One evening he spotted a mule deer
ambling up a hillside path
and he followed it to higher ground
as a huge moon rose off the ridge
and he caught the scent of pine needles.
So he kept on until dark, reaching a ledge
overlooking Phantom Lake and the ghost town.
His breath fogged in the cooling mountain air.
Moonlight seemed to pour from his nostrils.
He made camp there, sleeping that night
in a mess of dreams, troubled with bat squeaks,
with wild burros braying along the nearby creek.

At dawn the bats were pocketed upside down
in hollows of the canyon wall rinsing in pink light
and he saw the burros grazing wheatgrass and sage.
At the canyon head, a cave yawned open
but empty of the voices that muttered in the night.
And the blasted tree, high on the mesa rim
—that writhed at dusk like a man crucified—
was a tree again, rocking in the wind.
Stars gone, the sky streaked in sunlight.
A canyon wren, perched in a willow,
plied the dawn with inquiring song.

Be as careful of the end as you were of the beginning.

Tao Tê Ching, Chapter 64

ABOUT THE AUTHOR

John Balaban is the author of twelve books of poetry and prose, including four volumes which together received the Academy of American Poets' Lamont prize, a National Poetry Series Selection, and two nominations for the National Book Award. His *Locusts at the Edge of Summer: New & Selected Poems* won the 1998 William Carlos Williams Award from the Poetry Society of America. He was the 2001–2004 National Artist for the Phi Kappa Phi Honor Society. In 2003, he was awarded a Guggenheim Fellowship.

In addition to writing poetry, fiction, and nonfiction, he is a translator of Vietnamese poetry, and in 2008 he received a medal from the Vietnamese Ministry of Culture for his work in the digital preservation of ancient manuscripts and libraries. In 2017, he was given the George Garrett Award by the Association of Writers and Writing Programs.

Poetry is vital to language and living. Since 1972, Copper Canyon Press has published extraordinary poetry from around the world to engage the imaginations and intellects of readers, writers, booksellers, librarians, teachers, students, and donors.

WE ARE GRATEFUL FOR THE MAJOR SUPPORT PROVIDED BY:

THE PAUL G. ALLEN
FAMILY FOUNDATION

Anonymous

Jill Baker and Jeffrey Bishop

Anne and Geoffrey Barker

Donna and Matt Bellew

John Branch

Diana Broze

The Beatrice R. and Joseph A. Coleman Foundation Inc.

The Currie Family Fund

Laurie and Oskar Eustis

Mimi Gardner Gates

Nancy Gifford

Gull Industries Inc. on behalf of William True

The Trust of Warren A. Gummow

Carolyn and Robert Hedin

Bruce Kahn

Phil Kovacevich and Eric Wechsler

Lakeside Industries Inc.
on behalf of Jeanne Marie Lee

TO LEARN MORE ABOUT UNDERWRITING
COPPER CANYON PRESS TITLES,
PLEASE CALL 360-385-4925 EXT. 103

WE ARE GRATEFUL FOR THE MAJOR SUPPORT PROVIDED BY:

Maureen Lee and Mark Busto
Peter Lewis
Ellie Mathews and Carl Youngmann as The North Press
Hank Meijer
Gregg Orr
Petunia Charitable Fund and adviser Elizabeth Hebert
Gay Phinny
Suzie Rapp and Mark Hamilton
Emily and Dan Raymond
Jill and Bill Ruckelshaus
Cynthia Sears
Kim and Jeff Seely
Richard Swank
Dan Waggoner
Barbara and Charles Wright
Caleb Young as C. Young Creative
The dedicated interns and faithful volunteers
of Copper Canyon Press

The Chinese character for poetry is made up of two parts:
"word" and "temple."
It also serves as pressmark for Copper Canyon Press.

This book is set in Joanna.
Design by Katy Homans.
Printed on archival-quality paper.